The Sleepwalker's Memoirs

Moving Through the Darkness

Michaela Hackman

Copyright © 2016 by Michaela Hackman

All rights reserved. No part of this book may be reproduced or transmitted in any form or by any means, electronic or mechanical, including photocopying, recording, or by any information storage and retrieval system without the written permission of the author, except where permitted by law.

Any resemblance to actual persons, living or dead, or actual events in this work of poetry and prose is purely coincidental.

Printed in the U.S.A.

Sometimes you awake from a dream
Wonder where you are
And realize you were sleeping

Sometimes you awake from sleeping
Wonder where you are
And realize you weren't living

Michaela Hackman

Michaela Hackman

A Man Without A Soul

Would you recognize a man without a soul?
Will you see the emptiness in his eyes
The coldness in his touch
Do you think that your heart could survive?

He'll sweep you off of your feet
He'll suck you in and love you fast
Make you feel like you're queen of his world
You won't realize how much time has passed

He'll tell you he can't live without you
Set you up on an imaginary pedestal
But will you realize that the price for that
Will be the part of you that he stole?

He'll act confused
If you try to explain how hurt you feel
Wonder why you need so much
And treat you like this wasn't a part of the deal

You buy his lines because you wonder
Your self-esteem left you unsure
Why should he think so much of you?
You no longer remember

The girl you were before

A simple request that he speak the truth
Will have him twist your words
To make you weak
His story will change like the wind
But he will steadfastly believe no lies he speaks

Because when you're weak
He can mold you to his needs
He will ignore your pleads
He will have planted the seeds

To be king of his world
And you to be his servant
After a while
You begin to believe you deserve it

Confidence in yourself is stripped
You only want to keep the peace
You suppress your own needs
By keeping tight lipped
Wishing for arguments you can't win to cease

It becomes your job to make him happy
When he's happy he loves you

And when he loves you
Leaving him is that last thing you want to do

Until the lies start over again
And he points the blame on you
All the while charming everyone around him
Holding you hostage
But nothing is new

Then one day you need him
Sadness fills your eyes
He looks at you with emptiness
He can no longer disguise

The lack of compassion in his heart
You realize then that it was never there
And sadness fills your soul because
You finally see that he never cared

You begin to build a wall
To protect your pride
Because he will only make you
Feel shame inside

He'll manipulate you into believing
He's the best you're capable of receiving

You're invisible to him
Unless you put him first
He shows everyone his best
He gives you his worst

You can't quite put a finger
On how it all went so wrong
You keep hoping he'll change
But keep moving along

Hoping one day he will wake up and realize
How much he has to gain
If he would only care about
Something other than his name

But the truth is someone without a soul
Can never see anything other than
How he wants to be
And expects everyone around him
To comply with his needs

He'll charm you 'til he hooks you
Until one day you realize
You've been such a fool
To be in love with a man without a soul

~~~~~~~~~~~~

She looked back over the years and wondered how she arrived to this. It seemed cliché to her to think that there comes a time when, after everything you hoped for dies, you awaken with new purpose.

She never would have imagined spending so many years in isolation. She felt very alone, yet she wasn't alone. But no longer recognized the man she stood next to. Did she ever really know him?

She had reached her breaking point. This forward motion had to stop before it destroyed her. She could no longer fool herself into believing anything would ever change.

~~~~~~~~~~~~

Forgiveness

Forgiveness
But I don't remember
Hearing you say you're sorry
I'm supposed to grant this to you just because?

I let you stomp on me
And I tell you it hurts
But you never say you are sorry

Your excuses cast blame
As if somehow I asked for it
You make me feel the shame
And cover it up for no one to see
How black and blue inside you made me

But maybe I did ask for it
Simply by being weak enough
To let someone like you in my life

Someone who shields their own insecurities
By pointing out others'
Someone who lifts themselves up
By pushing down a brother

For too long I lived half alive

Not even realizing how much of me had died
Until one day I had nothing more to give
And I didn't care if tomorrow I lived

I awoke from that slumber in time
To realize that my life is mine
And it is time to close that door
On a life not worth living anymore

Forgiveness
You didn't ask me to forgive you
But I'm granting it to you anyway
Not because I approve of how you treat me
But because I want peace in my life
And I want to be free

Free from your words that cut like a knife
And the twisted and manipulative life
I felt forced to choose
But now I'll happily lose

Forgiveness
I forgive you
For being blissfully unaware
Of how insensitive you are
To the existence of others

And I pray for you
That one day you'll feel contrition in your heart
Before your empty soul breaks apart
Leaving you bitter and alone

Forgiveness
For my sake
Not yours

~~~~~~~~~~~~~

Michaela Hackman

Windbreaker

Your words are shallow...
Like the wind
That can't be captured and described

Your words have no meaning...
But can be felt
Like the treacherous force of a hurricane
When you speak

All that is left when you stop
Is the damage left behind...
Ripped hearts...
Tattered souls...

I need to find a soft breeze
With gentle words
That blow through my hair...
Tickles my skin...
Enlightens my soul...
Warms my heart...

I can't change the force with which you blow

It's time to put on my windbreaker
It's time for me to go

~~~~~~~~~~~~

The Tree

Do you see me?
Or am I invisible?

Like the tree
You hardly see
That stands here faithfully
Changing seasons always the same
Losing pieces only in storms

I'm here to shelter you
With shade from the burning sun
You hesitate to pick me up when I fall
Even though there are times I cannot help it at all

Left feeling invisible
I lie dormant in wintery discontent
Until I find a glimmer of hope
That makes me want to bloom again

You needing me
So you breathe life into me
But still not really seeing me

If you could only see
Every time you look at me
The beauty I bring to your life
Like the petals of blooms on a spring tree

If you could only see
Every time you look at me
The light that glimmers in my eyes
The way the sun gleams from the sky
Through leaves of a tree on a summer's day

If you could only see
Every time you look at me
All the colors of my love
Given to you bountifully
Like the majestic leaves
As they fall from trees

If you could only see
Every time you look at me
The coldness in my solitude
The brittleness in my spirit

As I await
For you to notice that I am here
Like a tree in winter
Ready to bloom once more

Before I become a hollow core

The Sleepwalker's Memoirs

She recalled the past and how they worked through a few rocky months, then another drama would begin. She would tell him to leave. Only she wasn't strong enough to resist his manipulation.

His smooth talk about how he promised to be a better man, promised to love and cherish her, promise to put her and the children first was all she needed to hear.

She believed him because he would look her straight in the eyes and tell her these things. She thought for sure she would know if he was lying. He had two personalities; who he really was, and who he pretended to be in order to be admired and loved.

Believing she didn't deserve any better, her self-confidence was shattered. She would take him back, and for the next few years stood on the edge, never sure which way she was about to fall.

~~~~~~~~~~~~

Frozen Suspension

The water flows past me
And I feel it try to push me over
Telling me to wake up
Forcing me to move

But I sit in frozen suspension
Not quite on the ground
But not floating up high either
I don't want to return
To where I was
But I don't know how to move on

I keep waiting…
Waiting for the right flow to come by
To pick me up and carry me
To where I want to be

But will I recognize the right flow?
Will I go in the right direction?
I'm afraid of trying
Afraid of getting it wrong

It's easier to do nothing
And sit in frozen suspension

*I see a space ahead
And I want to explore it
But it feels so far away
And I still feel unsure
Of where I belong*

*If I'm not welcomed
I'll feel rejected
And if it's not quite what I expected
I may accept it as an alternative
To where I was before
And feel stuck in a circular pool of discontent
As if somehow I don't deserve more
So I sit in frozen suspension*

*I want to believe that when my
Heart, mind, and soul
Work together
They will not deceive me
But in the meantime I'm missing out
On all there is to be*

*And I watch the raging water that flows
To places unknown
Wishing I was going too
Wishing I was already there*

I keep trying to find the strength to go
To follow the falls
To move on my own
And trust that any path is better
Than the one I had known

And I tell myself
To find my own path to flow
And to remember now I'm free
Because life will only bypass me
If I stay here in frozen suspension

She remembers when she died inside. His overly high sense of self-importance caused his ego to be attacked once again. He came home with the same old song and dance drama. A lost job, disgruntled with someone, a feeling of being done wrong.

It didn't matter which one this time, it was always something. This was not the first time. Instead of taking a hard look, humbly, at himself, he only knew how to belittle those who caused his ills. It was always someone else's fault. It was at that moment she felt absolutely defeated.

She remembers thinking to herself; "This is it. This is as good as it gets. This is my life, I made this bed, and now I need to lie in it."

She couldn't deny it any longer. She had been embraced by empty arms, with hands clasped in a firm grip that were not about to be easily released.

She prayed for him to be the man she needed him to be.

~~~~~~~~~~~~

Narcissist

Never did I think our paths would cross
All alone all the while you are here
Rarely feeling a presence not cold as stone
Crying would be a waste of tears
Inside you a void, an empty soul
Still others are fooled by your charm
Slowly my spirit breaks from your embrace
I die inside, but you think you've done no harm
Suffocating my love, my wants, and my needs
Tearing apart my heart as you watch me bleed

Today is a new day
Saving myself to redeem my soul
Inside new hope begins
Seeking reward for a paid toll
Sure of a past I must leave behind
I move forward with brand new eyes
Creating my own warm sunshine
Realizing I no longer need this disguise
Allowing myself to unload this past
Now and forever, I'm free at last

~~~~~~~~~~~~

Michaela Hackman

Out of the Darkness

I'm keeping his secret
I'm covering his tracks
The life you see him live
Is nothing but an act

His eyes stare with coldness
Of a bitter winter day
His heart is hard as stone
He knows no other way

His soul is as empty
As the captured wind
His mind works to convince me
Until my broken soul caves in

The walls of solitude bear heavy
Crumbling all around
I stand alone and scream
But no one hears a sound

My might to fight must come within
My own soul I must save
I stand firm and tall, I am done with it all
Now I know I am brave

From the cave into the wind
I cast out all the stone
I venture out into the spring
Renewed and alone

Out of the darkness I exit
My soul forever free
I head to all that awaits
And begin my search for me

~~~~~~~~~~~~

Gaslight

You distorted my reality
You wanted me to see
...what you believed true
...how you wanted it to be

Torched by lies
The truth was nowhere to be found
Words of honor
Lay as ashes on the ground

I won't believe your truth any longer
Your reality isn't mine anymore
Don't tell me how to think or feel
Take your flame throwing words
And walk out that door

She thought back to the day she met him. He was funny, cute, bold, and confident. He seemed enthralled by her. Their dating life was fun, exciting, and filled with new experiences.

The voice inside of her kept screaming, "He's not for you! Don't get caught up in him!" But she ignored that voice. That is exactly what he wanted.

Reliving that time in her mind makes her think about a bug being caught in a spider web, but at the time she thought it was a maze of wonderment and love.

Everything had moved too fast. Her life was in a vortex, and she didn't know how to slow it down. She wasn't sure at that time if she really wanted it to slow down.

She didn't realize, or perhaps in her loneliness had forgotten, that a foundation of true love and caring is built over time. She accepted the accelerated overinflated infatuation as love. She didn't see the signs. Her feet weren't planted firmly enough to see that she was his prey.

~~~~~~~~~~~~

Michaela Hackman

Web of Lies

Oh the tangled webs you weaved…
The truth would slip right by
And be lost in a tangled web of lies
Leaving an unanswered why
In the tangled webs you weaved

You were the weaver…
Standing back to claim your fame
Pointing fingers to lay blame
If someone tried to test your name
In the tangled webs you weaved

But you weren't the one getting caught up…
You made it easy to deceive
Hiding the truth you were able to achieve
From anyone willing to believe
In the tangled webs you weaved

You weaved a web of deception…
I was caught up in your deceit
Confused by charm shown to people you meet
They were blind to your conceit
And to the tangled webs you weaved

Not knowing the truth anymore...
Your web choked me from my voice
Making me think I had no choice
In my sorrow you rejoiced
In the tangled webs you weaved

Oh the tangled webs you weaved

Until I learned to take that web
And spin it like thread
And forget everything you said

I finally saw the truth
Never again to be deceived
From your lies I have been freed
With this silk armor suit that I have weaved

From the tangled webs you used to weave

~~~~~~~~~~~~

Michaela Hackman

Shattered Glass

*All around me lay fragments of my life
Shattered pieces of glass that represent
Dreams, hopes, promises, love
Broken in strife*

*Everything I had ever wanted
Lay in pieces on the ground
I tried so hard to pick up those pieces
And put them back together
But the fractures stuck around*

*I would be cut sharply from my attempts
Bleeding only more each time
The weakened structure would quickly break
Creating a new paradigm*

*I don't know how to make this reminder
Of my failures go away
I try to walk away from it, but it follows me
I try to sweep it up, but it stays*

*I don't know what to do
With all of these fragments of glass
I don't want to continue
to be followed by my past*

I start to move the pieces around
Mixing the broken promises
With the crushed dreams
Shattered hope, shredded love

The light from above reflects
On the different colors of the mixed glass
And I no longer see what they were in my past
New images are now in my sight
I see them shine in a new light

I stir the pieces again and it shows me more
I vaguely remember
How the glass came to be broken before

The excitement of the new images it gives me
Is greater than the sorrow
Of how the broken glass came to be

I pick up the pieces
Making them into something meaningful to me
Creating new hopes
Dreams
Promises
Love

And free the path around me
With wounds healed

But scars that serve only as a reminder
Of how far I've come
Of how strong I am
How much I can endure
And how much I have won

~~~~~~~~~~~~

Leaving him wasn't going to be easy. He tried his best to bring her down to a very painful, emotional level, slicing her to her core with his temper and his choice of words. It was a fragile place to be. Her sense of safety was gone. But, then she thought, was she ever safe in his world?

She knew his lack of compassion and self-centeredness would keep turning to rage, but there was no way to prepare for such verbal abuse.

She knew she could no longer just keep the peace; she walked on eggshells in order to do so. She gave up so much of herself living for him. Her love for him wasn't going to save him, nor would it ever change him.

Michaela Hackman

See Who They Are

How do you stop hoping
For someone to be who you want them to be
And start accepting them
For who they are

When you know
If you had to open your eyes
To see who they really are

You're not sure
You could be around them
Without feeling

Hurt
Rejected
Insignificant

So instead
You keep looking
For glimmers of hope
That they are who you want them to be

Keep twisting every sign
Into what you want to see
Blinding yourself

*Until it hurts
And you feel rejected
And appear insignificant
Anyway*

*Believe them
When they show you
Who they are
If they won't change for themselves
They will never change for you*

~~~~~~~~~~~~

What Are You Waiting For

What are you waiting for?

What do you expect to see changed?

You're not in control of much

Except your destiny you arrange

When you keep thinking you're not worthy

You'll be led down the wrong path

Fakeness all around you

Broken pieces in the aftermath

He would not let up his approach to reconcile. He would plead his case, saying he loved her and wanted to make it work.

He would say that he loved her so much it hurt. He claimed that all he ever did was love her too much, that they could work this out and be a family again.

She would insist that there was nothing to talk about, reminding him that he has lied over and over. He would steadfastly deny any wrongdoing.

The pleas would turn to angry, hurtful words spewed with hate meant to scare her into compliance. She had to stay strong all the while trying to minimize escalating his rage.

He would try to discredit her to anyone who would listen.

The answers to her prayers weren't appearing in the form of him being the man she needed him to be. The answer was in showing her the man he clearly was, and in showing her the path leading the way out.

Cries of a Broken Soul

If the broken soul of a woman
Cries out in the middle of a crowded room
Does anybody hear her?

No
Because she hides it

She wakes each day
Paints on a perfect smile
Disguises the pain in her eyes
Brushes the dust off of her soul
Closes off her rusty heart
And walks out into the world

She watches as others
Are nourished with
Hope
Love
Dreams

She wants to eat that fruit
But it seems so out of reach
A garden not of her own

She moves through her day
Hungry

Thirsty
Longing for the fruit others know

Those who see her
Think she's fine
It's that disguise
They can't see behind

Only
She knows how it feels
To be malnourished
Uncherished

She stands and screams
But the disguise she wears
Muffles the sound
Others only hear the voice
Of beauty and strength

As she ends her day
She removes the disguise
Lays in her bed and cries
Hoping tomorrow will be different

But when tomorrow comes
Will she have strength
To no longer disguise the feelings inside

And look into the mirror
To see her inner beauty
Flow out through her tears
To wash away all the fears
And walk out into the world
Strong enough to nourish herself
No longer feeling the need to scream

Eating the fruit of
Hope
Love
Dreams
One bite at a time
From a garden she planted
Fruits of a life sublime

Blind

I couldn't see in front of me
Blind and alone I wandered through the days
A drug I didn't mean to take
I walked confused and dazed

Stay or go
Go or stay
A choice
I'd end up choosing wrong

Highs and lows
Lows and high
The good too short
The bad lasts too long

What's blinding me!
I scream
Why can't I see my worth!
Not how my life was meant to be
It's time for a rebirth

No rehab as the cure
No pills to ease the pain
I must find the strength within
Or risk staying insane

The task is not easy
As I claw at what makes me blind
And replace the empty sockets
With new vision and a clear mind

Breathe in
Breathe out
And blink
See a new sun rise
And move towards the life I seek
Move forward with new eyes.

~~~~~~~~~~~~~

She thinks about her path in life, and wonders what it would be like if she made different choices.

Who would she be now?

She felt an emptiness; a lack of fulfillment and passion so desired. She considers that having made any other choice would've required knowing herself, and loving herself first.

She wonders how can she look in the mirror and see the reflection of a woman with a lifetime ahead of her filled with joy, love, and beauty; when all of the sadness, shame, and ugliness still lingers in the background.

Now is the time to let it go.

She knows she must fill that emptiness herself. To do so would start with new sight; seeing her own worth.

~~~~~~~~~~~~

Forgiving Myself

I remain my own worst enemy
There are many who stand by
Ready to persecute me
But I have beaten them to it

I never let myself off the hook
For my imperfections
I never relieve myself
From the objections in my head
That tell me I must be perfect

I create my own prison
And the wound it causes
Is an incision in my mind
That makes me think I'm not good enough

I'm locked in purgatory on earth
Questioning my own self worth
Like I'm some currency that can be exchanged

Right for wrong
Good for bad
Weak for strong

I won't give myself a break

Michaela Hackman

From the paths that I take
But why can't I see
That I'm expecting way too much of me

This perfection is only a reflection
Of my own self image
That hides behind the fear of failure

Failure weighs me down
And I feel like I will drown
From the pressures I place on myself

Mixing the signals of failure with sin
Instead of failure leads to a win
When I can learn from my mistakes
And not repeat them

I go to war with myself each day
For the decisions I made
That didn't lead the way to the life I expected

The shadow boxing leaves me bruised
Confused
And used
As I serve as my own judge and jury

Why can't I find it in me to forgive myself

To gently take my tattered heart off the shelf
And let it beat again

Why do I carry this burden of guilt
That is over a bridge that I built
When no one that matters
Is forcing me to do so

Why don't I just burn this bridge
Soften my soul with edges ridged
Set my mind and body free
From these chains that bind me

And forgive myself
Take the key from the shelf
Unlock this prison door
Free from expectations of more

Let go of what I can't control
Be gentle on my caring soul

Learn to take each moment as it comes
And admire the woman I've become

I will never be able to let the past be
And move to the future that I want to see
Until I am able to forgive me

Michaela Hackman

A Coloring Book Life

We grow up in a world
With coloring books on a shelf
We're expected to choose one
Designed by someone else

A standard issue box of crayons
A rainbow of colors
Color inside the lines
Vivid and bright
And be like all the others

But it's all so one dimensional
Over time the colors fade
The lines blur
Our dreams go away

I went back to the shelf
To find something new
The first one I had chosen
Left me blank
Empty
Blue

I stood there flipping pages
Not seeing what I wanted to see

*I realized these books weren't meant
To let me be who I wanted to be*

*I left that shelf and searched
For a notebook
Clean and clear
And decided from that day on
I'll make my own pages appear*

Michaela Hackman

Perfect Picture

That perfect picture on the wall
All that life is supposed to be?
I look beyond the picture
My real life is what I see

I kept trying to frame pictures
Perfect times to make them stay
The harder I seemed to try
The more I got in my own way

Life is like a series of puzzles
All the time ever changing
The pieces change
The pictures change
It's never meant for framing

I don't want my life stuck
Behind a glass and frame
I'll never change, I'll never grow
My life will stay the same

Pieces of a puzzle
With no finished picture to see
Leaves me with hope and wonder
Of how great my life can be

~~~~~~~~~~~~

She recognizes how to not fall into the same trap again. Unhealthy behaviors are more obvious now, but she still must guard her heart. Learning to trust again will be a process.

She doesn't want to spend the rest of her life alone. She already spent too many years alone. Alone, while living with a man who knew nothing about her, who wasn't interested in her, and who's only interest in her was directly related to how happy she made him.

Of course he "loved" her, she did everything she could to make him happy. It was always about him. But she never felt loved.

He had a sense of entitlement that was insatiable. He needed her for his very survival, but treated her like she was the reason for everything that went wrong.

She never felt like she was "enough", and always wondered why he wasn't interested in her. "What is wrong with me?" She wondered. "Why am I not enough?"

~~~~~~~~~~~~

Magnificently Imperfect

He judged my soul
Without ever showing his own
Not enough
Never enough
What is enough?

Enough!
Taking the gavel back into my own hands
I tapped his skin to awaken his soul
But he shattered into a million pieces
Revealing his nothingness
His emptiness

I swept up only the pieces of myself
He had chipped away and taken from me
Carefully discarding those I no longer needed
Placing back those I had missed
Making new ones
To complete the puzzle I had become

In a new light I awoke
To ever changing color and reflection
In each perfectly crafted piece
Creating a magnificently imperfect me

~~~~~~~~~~~~

The Sleepwalker's Memoirs

Michaela Hackman

Searching For My Twin

Excuse me Sir, can you help me?
I'm looking for my twin
I haven't seen her in many years
I don't even know where to begin

What's that, you ask? Can I describe her?
Well, she stands about this tall
In the summer her hair is a bit light blond
But it's back to brown by fall

She has kind eyes and a warm heart
And is a bit funny in a sarcastic way
She can cook
She can clean
She can climb a mountain top
And do it all in a day

She's a friend
She's a giver, never a taker
She would never want to break a heart
She works hard
Takes pride
Excels in all that she does
She finishes all that she starts

She left a long time ago…
Well actually no, that isn't true

Her body was here going through the motions
But her soul was black and blue

She has achieved much success in the world
But there's one thing she still seeks to find
And that's what it feels like to be deeply loved
Body, soul and mind

So, kind Sir, can you help?
Have you seen my twin?
The man held up a mirror and said
"Who you seek is there, within

For if you care enough about the world
And all that is in it
The love you seek will find you
Once you believe you deserve to be in it

So I say to you, dear girl, dear twin
You're one, you are the same
Once you see the best in her is YOU
You will have your flame

Your flame will burn with fire
Lit from passion in your soul
Love will be drawn to your warmth
As you will have paid your toll

When you know your own true worth
You will attract the right kind

Don't settle for less than someone
Who will love you
Body, soul and mind.

So don't give up, dear girl
Take this mirror to help you see
The wonderful woman looking back
And know that you are free"

She realizes the paths people take in life are sometimes so bumpy that even the best of intentions, the love in the deepest depths of our heart, can still lead to heartbreak and loneliness.

Maybe the path that she set out on was meant to lead her right where she is today; with all the bumps, bruises, and baggage; to give her the opportunity to finally know what she is made of.

She has it within herself to change that path.

She faces each new experience head on. Sometimes with fear, sometimes with grace, but always with her eyes wide open.

With each step forward, she finds herself looking ahead, and putting the past behind without looking back.

There is a whole world of possibilities.

Each day is a new opportunity to grow, to learn, to hope.

~~~~~~~~~~

Michaela Hackman

Illusion of the Tunnel

The illusion of the light at the end of the tunnel
Keeps us from leaving that never ending funnel
We keep seeking the end to accept the light
Looking around with blinded sight

When all along the real resistance
In ever reaching that imaginary distance
Is our own fear of imagination
Dreams fraught with endless frustration

The light at the end can never be reached
The tunnel walls upon our lives are leached
But in fact the barrier doesn't exist at all
The real illusion is the tunnel walls

~~~~~~~~~~~~

Battles of the Past

Leave the past behind
No need to make it disappear
Take strength
Wisdom
And peace from the past
Hold on to all that is dear

One day you'll look upon
Just how far you've come
And smile at the very thought
Of the battles you have won

Move on into the future
Let darkness cast upon the past
Live a life filled with brightness
And joy will forever last

~~~~~~~~~~~~

Michaela Hackman

Rain

The rain falls
Cascading from angry clouds
Floating in the sky

Beads of water releasing
Fear
Sadness
Uncertainty

Transformed mid-air
Soaking into the ground
Into my heart
Into my soul
All around me

Bringing life back into my being
Fear washes away
Sadness drowns
New life blossoms in my soul
Colors once faded bloom
Certainty returns

The rain falls
Making all things new again

~~~~~~~~~~~~

The road ahead is clear.

She has fallen back onto land and crawled from the edge, far enough away to safely get up and walk. She knows her direction, and knows she is strong enough to not turn back.

She won't live for him anymore.

She now stands at the beginning of the new road, and with each step finds herself moving away from pain, moving towards joy.

She spent many years trying to make everyone else happy, doing for everyone else, and equating her happiness to the ability to make others happy.

Finding herself along the way, she looks at each new day with appreciation.

Expectations

Expectations
Like paper wings
Tear in the wind
Flutter in the breeze
While lifted off the ground
Unsteady
Unstable
Whirling here and there

Appreciation
Forms wings made of silk
Strong against the gust
Moves straight through the gale
Able to stand firm
Safe
Solid
Enduring only what is true

~~~~~~~~~~~~

Along the way she has come to realize that friendship, family, and love relationships are all the same; it is a two way street.

She will bend over backwards for someone; but now has learned to accept that same gift from those willing to do the same for her, and to stop bending so much for those who won't.

She made the decision soon after to let down the walls she had built, and not be afraid to let people get close.

Allowing herself to feel vulnerable was foreign to her, but in order to heal, she must. This time, she knows her worth.

A Message From Those Who Truly Love You

If I gave you my eyes would you see
The beauty in you that I see
Would you look at the world with amazement
And use your new vision to be free

From the discontent in your sight
As you see it now
It holds you back from living
Unhappiness screaming loud

If I gave you my heart would you feel
Love for yourself as I do
Tenderness, kindness, and peace
All the feelings that are true

Warmth to wrap yourself in love
To keep you safe and content
The love my heart will give you
In abundance will be sent

So if you struggle much to see
When you look into the mirror
All the beauty you bring into this world

Please don't ever fear

Reach out to those who love you
Ask them for their eyes
Borrow their heart for a moment
The feeling may come as a surprise

Embrace that time forever
Because this is what truth is
A moment with those who love you
Are moments meant to live

The journey continues, and she has moments when she thinks about the time wasted. Questioning why she didn't act sooner.

Then there are other moments when she realizes how lucky she was not to have wasted one more day in such a hopeless situation.

She remembers the day she came back to life. The process of awakening was long, and was filled with relief, despair, joy, and pain.

At first the despair and pain was heavy, with an occasional glimpse of relief and joy. Then slowly over time the relief and joy began to outpace the despair and pain.

She liked the woman she was becoming. Stronger, more capable, more appreciative of her own worth. Moving past the pain and into a new dawn gave her life back.

This time, she's writing the chapters, and drawing the pictures along the way.

~~~~~~~~~~~

Michaela Hackman

The New Dawn

The morning offers the song it sings
Showing possibility of what today will bring
I see the night clouds break away
The sun burning to make a new day

Clouds form like mountain top peaks
Laced with yellow and gold
As the sun shamelessly seeks
Making way for blue skies and a new dawn
The last of night forever gone

What will I do with this new chance I'm given
The ills of yesterday must be forgiven
For today is full of possibility to strive
To be the best I can be and be grateful I'm alive

When each morning offers a fresh new start
May I face it ready to do my part
And grace the world with the best of me
And encourage others to see what I see

A world of hope, of faith, and of love
The beauty of life given from God above

~~~~~~~~~~~~

A flower blooms
Her true color unknown
Until she knows herself

The End

. . .actually, it's only the beginning

ABOUT THE AUTHOR

Michaela Hackman is a native of Latrobe, Pennsylvania and currently resides in the upstate of South Carolina. Her dream when she was 10 years old was to travel the world to take pictures and write stories. Long ago she put down the pen, picking it up 25 years later with the compassion and grace of a woman who has seen the world, both the good and the bad. Her poetry symbolizes the search for being true to one's self. Her writing is intended to help ordinary people to find hope, and to not feel so alone as they struggle to deal with obstacles in their lives.

www.ingramcontent.com/pod-product-compliance
Lightning Source LLC
Chambersburg PA
CBHW071412040426
42444CB00009B/2215